OUR WORLD IN COLOUR
TAJ MAHAL

TOUR WORLD IN COLOUR
TAJ MAHAL

Photographs by Satish Sharma
Text by Narayani Gupta

The Guidebook Company Limited

(title spread)
A skyline which has remained unchanged for three hundred years.

(right) *Like a page of an illustrated manuscript, Quranic verses frame the great central arch which leads the visitor to the Taj Mahal. The exuberant pietra dura, the geometrical designs which blend red sand-stone and black and white marble, and the row of miniature bulbous marble domes give a foretaste of the Taj Mahal.*

(pages 6-7)
The perfect proportions of the Taj conceal its great height (43 metres) and the balance is further enhanced by the mosque on the west (foreground) and the Mehman-Khana (assembly hall) on the east. The sandstone used for these offsets the white of the Taj in sharper relief. Shah Jahan is often said to have planned a mausoleum for himself in black marble on the opposite side of the River Yamuna.

(pages 8-9)
The entrance to a ghost city— the City of Victory (Fatehpur) built by Akbar and abandoned within a few years.

(pages 10-11)
Near Agra, at Sikandra, is the royal tomb of Akbar, the Mughal emperor. The gateway to the tomb is beautifully decorated with inlay work, marble and sandstone.

Text by Narayani Gupta
Photography by Satish Sharma
and Fredrik Arvidsson 10-11, 25 (left), 27, 38-9, 41, 46 (bottom), 47 49 (bottom), 51, 53, 55, 70-1, 73 (top), 75, 80.
Old Photographs and prints on pages 23 (bottom), 29, 31 (top), 40 (both) and 50/51 courtesy of Toby Sinclair

Editor: David Clive Price
Series Editor: John Anthony Oliver
Designed by TC Design
Created by Gulmohur Press, New Delhi

Production House: Twin Age Ltd, Hong Kong

Printed in China

ISBN 962-217-130-3

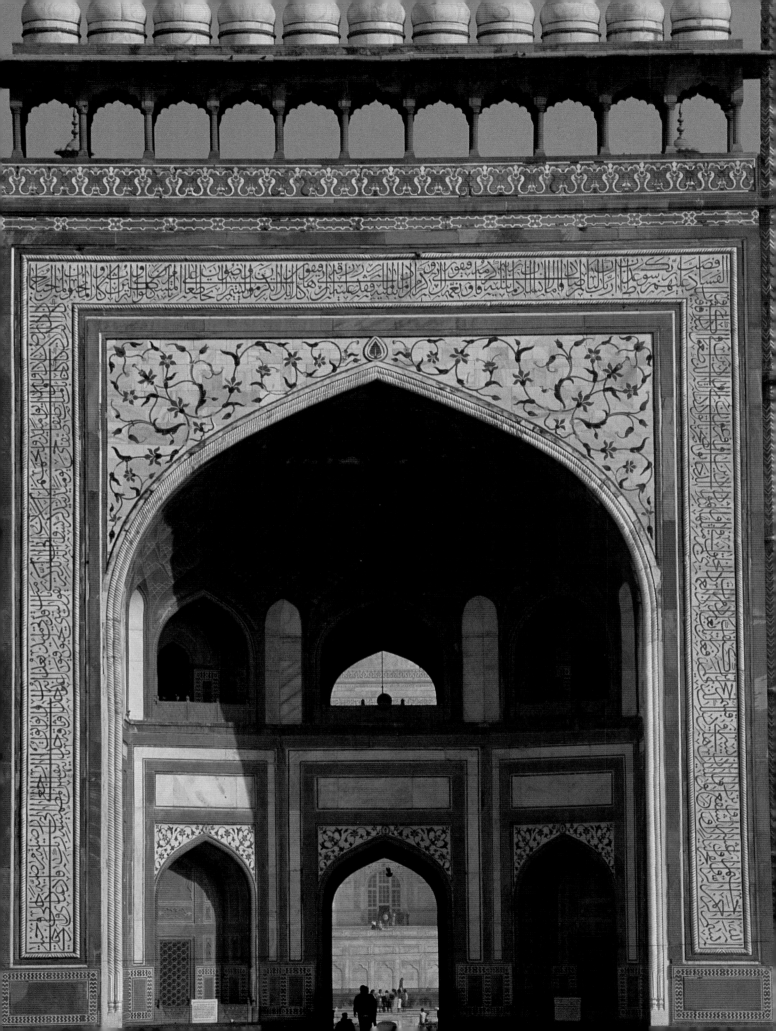

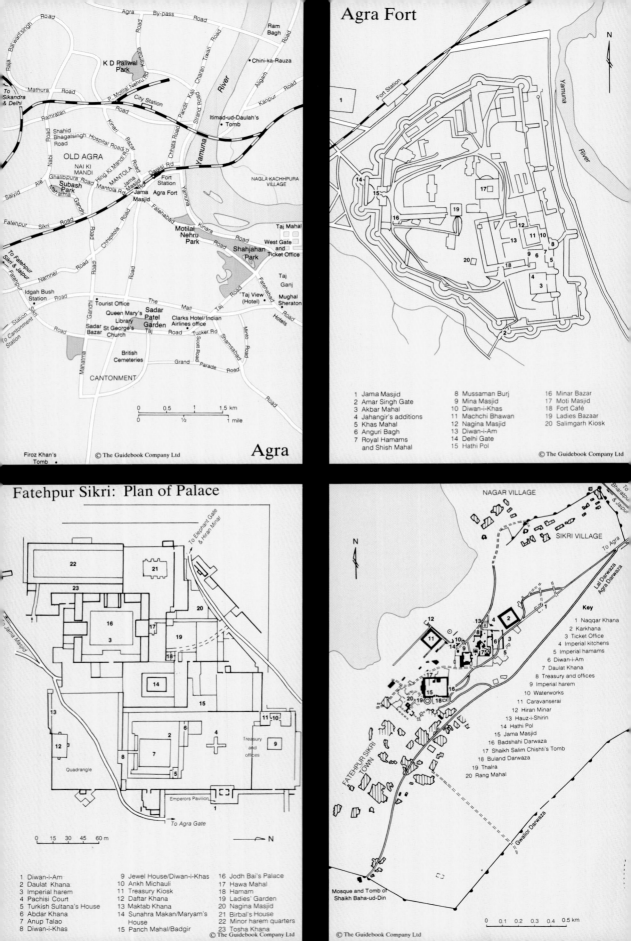

Agra

K D Paliwal Park

Chini-ka-Rauza •

River

Itimad-ud-Daulah's • Tomb

OLD AGRA
NAI KI MANDI
Subash Park

NAGLA KACHHPURA VILLAGE

Jama Masjid

Agra Fort

Fort Station

Motilal Nehru Park

Shahjahan Park

West Gate and Ticket Office

Taj Mahal

Taj Ganj

Mughal Sheraton

Taj View (Hotel)

Hotels

Idgah Bush Station

Tourist Office
Queen Mary's Library
Sadar Patel Garden
Clarks Hotel/Indian Airlines office

Sadar Bazar
St George's Church

British Cemeteries

CANTONMENT

To Sikandra & Delhi

To Fatehpur Sikri & Jaipur

Firoz Khan's Tomb

| 0 | 0.5 | 1 | 1.5 km |
| 0 | ½ | | 1 mile |

© The Guidebook Company Ltd

Agra Fort

N

Yamuna River

Fort Station

1 Jama Masjid
2 Amar Singh Gate
3 Akbar Mahal
4 Jahangir's additions
5 Khas Mahal
6 Anguri Bagh
7 Royal Hamams and Shish Mahal
8 Mussaman Burj
9 Mina Masjid
10 Diwan-i-Khas
11 Machchi Bhawan
12 Nagina Masjid
13 Diwan-i-Am
14 Delhi Gate
15 Hathi Pol
16 Minar Bazar
17 Moti Masjid
18 Fort Café
19 Ladies Bazaar
20 Salimgarh Kiosk

© The Guidebook Company Ltd

Fatehpur Sikri: Plan of Palace

To Elephant Gate & Hiran Minar

To Jama Masjid

Quadrangle

Treasury and offices

Emperor's Pavilion

To Agra Gate

| 0 | 15 | 30 | 45 | 60 m |

N

1 Diwan-i-Am
2 Daulat Khana
3 Imperial harem
4 Pachisi Court
5 Turkish Sultana's House
6 Abdar Khana
7 Anup Talao
8 Diwan-i-Khas
9 Jewel House/Diwan-i-Khas
10 Ankh Michauli
11 Treasury Kiosk
12 Daftar Khana
13 Maktab Khana
14 Sunahra Makan/Maryam's House
15 Panch Mahal/Badgir
16 Jodh Bai's Palace
17 Hawa Mahal
18 Hamam
19 Ladies' Garden
20 Nagina Masjid
21 Birbal's House
22 Minor harem quarters
23 Tosha Khana

© The Guidebook Company Ltd

NAGAR VILLAGE

To Bharatpur & Jaipur

SIKRI VILLAGE

To Agra

Lal Darwaza
Agra Darwaza

FATEHPUR SIKRI TOWN

Key

1 Naqqar Khana
2 Karkhana
3 Ticket Office
4 Imperial kitchens
5 Imperial hamams
6 Diwan-i-Am
7 Daulat Khana
8 Treasury and offices
9 Imperial harem
10 Waterworks
11 Caravanserai
12 Hiran Minar
13 Hauz-i-Shirin
14 Hathi Pol
15 Jama Masjid
16 Badshahi Darwaza
17 Shaikh Salim Chishti's Tomb
18 Buland Darwaza
19 Thalra
20 Rang Mahal

Gwalior Darwaza

Mosque and Tomb of Shaikh Baha-ud-Din

| 0 | 0.1 | 0.2 | 0.3 | 0.4 | 0.5 km |

© The Guidebook Company Ltd

INTRODUCTION

AROUND the time of the French Revolution, two British artists, Thomas Daniell and his nephew William, were scrambling up the dome of what they called the 'Tage Mahl'. 'It has always been considered as the first example of Mahomedan architecture in India and consequently, being a spectacle of the highest celebrity, is visited by persons of all rank, and from all arts,' they wrote. 'This high admiration is however not confined to the partial eye of the native Indian; it is beheld with no less wonder and delight by those who have seen the productions of art in various parts of the globe.' (J. Mahajan, *Pictuesque India*, New Delhi, 1983) The spirit of Emperor Shah Jahan would be gladdened to know that for thousands of people the Taj Mahal he built is synonymous with Agra, even with India.

In 1643, the Taj Mahal was completed. It symbolised the emperor's great love for beautiful craftsmanship and elegant buildings, especially in marble, as well as his great love for his wife, Mumtaz Mahal, who had died tragically young. Few wives of the great have been thus commemorated. Many years later, Shah Jahan himself was laid to rest in the Taj Mahal, but it was originally built to fulfil a promise made at his wife's deathbed. For her he built the most perfectly designed mausoleum he could, a product of his own good taste and the talents of many craftsmen. And in so doing he lifted Agra from a position of faded grandeur to world-wide renown.

Agra

The hills and rivers of the Ganga-Yamuna plain are very old. For many centuries there have been towns here, sometimes large enough to be dignified by the term 'city'. Some were political capitals, others were shrines. Pilgrims to the holy towns of Mathura, Vrindavan, Banaras and Allahabad have worshipped the rivers and drawn sustenance from them for hundreds of years. The city of Agra is relatively young, or if it has an ancient pedigree, as Delhi has, we do not know it. From the 16th century on, Agra became a name on the map and acquired a regional primacy that it did not lose even when it ceased to be an imperial capital. Today's visitor sees a crowded city of some millions of inhabitants. At the core of it is Akbarabad, the capital named after the greatest Mughal emperor, known to us simply as Akbar (literally 'The Great').

From the 13th until the 15th century, Delhi was the chief city of Islamic South Asia. In the 16th century, people in Europe were puzzled to hear of another city, Agra. In 1505, the last-but-one of the Delhi sultans, Sikander Lodi, built a small fort in Agra, near which was a township named after him, Sikandra. A battle fought in 1526 at Panipat, many miles north of Delhi, ended the Lodi dynasty and introduced to India an elegant and witty man whom his followers called Babur (literally, 'The Tiger'). If rulers were judged not by the length of time they held on to their throne, or by the extent of their territory, but by how well their works endured, the three-century-long Timurid Dynasty (known by the somewhat confusing name 'Mughal') would get a high rating.

The searing heat and the dust of the plains of Hindustan (North India) oppressed but did not daunt people from the cooler regions of Central Asia. When Babur found it difficult to hold on to his throne in Ferghana (in Central Asia), he moved to Kabul and thence, following the steps of his ancestor, Timur, to North India. Once the exhilaration of his victory over Ibrahim Lodi abated, he was dismayed to see the spoils of his victory. What a country, he exclaimed, lacking in towns, gardens, melons and grapes, ice, and all the delights of urbane society! When someone brought him a musk-melon from Kabul, he became suddenly and desperately homesick. His followers too longed to return to Afghanistan. But Babur pulled

Few, if any, of the jalis, *or screens, follow the same design Most are carved out of a single slab of the finest marble or, in the case of Fatehpur Sikri, sandstone. While presenting a secure wall to the outside,* jalis *allow air to circulate and subdued light to enter the building.*

himself together and rallied his soldiers: 'What necessity has arisen that we should, without cause, abandon countries taken at such risk of life?' he demanded. Unlike Timur, therefore, Babur opted to stay in India. He did not live long enough to build a citadel, but he did the next best thing: on the bank of the Yamuna at Agra, he laid out a garden in the Persian *chahar-bagh* style. Here began a tradition that was to culminate four centuries later in Viceroy Hardinge asking the architect of New Delhi, Edwin Lutyens, to design a 'Mughal Garden' for the viceroy's palace. One of Babur's happy discoveries at Gwalior was the pink oleander. 'I took some to Agra,' he wrote, 'and had them planted in gardens there.' He bequeathed to his successors his love of the beautiful, his passion for birds and flowers, together with a small kingdom. He was buried at Agra, on the left bank of the Yamuna, but later his body was removed to a grave in Kabul, which he had wanted as his resting-place.

Babur's son, Humayun, led a charmed life. His father had drawn him out of an early illness, as the legend goes, by taking it on himself. Later, fleeing from the army of his formidable rival, Sher Shah Sur, he was saved by a water–carrier who Humayun gratefully installed for a few days on his throne at Delhi. When he was finally secure against all rivals, Humayun's luck ran out and he died as a result of stumbling down the steps of his library. In the course of his difficult life, his solace had been to dream of beautiful buildings nestling among lakes and groves. To him belongs the citadel in Delhi commonly known as the Purana Qila ('Old Fort'); near this is the mausoleum built for him by his widow—it is one of the most stupendous triumphs of Indian architecture. The marble and sandstone used for it was typical of later Mughal architecture: its design was a prototype of the Taj Mahal.

Babur and Humayun had come through much adversity; Akbar was born to it. When he was first saw life in the desert of Sind his impoverished father had only a pod of musk to give away to his followers as a token of joy. He did this with characteristic grace, and with the prayer that Akbar's fame would spread in the same way as did the fragrance of the musk. The prayer was answered. To an Indian schoolchild, Akbar shares with Ashok the honour of being one of the greatest rulers of India. His empire stretched from Afghanistan to Bengal, from Kashmir to Central India. But it is not the awesome size of his empire that people remember. Akbar is a legend because of his peaceful campaign against religious bigotry. In a period when many people were being persecuted in the name of religion (as in post-Reformation Europe), Akbar sought through his proclamation of a universalist creed to find a common ground between all faiths.

Akbar's anxiety to have an heir led him to seek the help of the saintly figure of Salim Chishti, who lived at Sikri, 23 miles (37 kilometres) west of Agra. When the son was born, the graceful emperor decided to build himself a capital near the Chishti shrine, a kind of Versailles to Agra's Paris. Chishti himself did not live to see the citadel, called by the triumphant name of Fatehabad ('City of Victory', signifying Akbar's conquest of the South); later it was modified to Fatehpur. Its elegant complex of sandstone building crowned the hill near the village of Sikri, and on the slope the nobles built their mansions. Babur had been amazed at the swiftness with which towns were built and abandoned in India. His grandson's city bore this out. The puzzle of why Fatehpur, which had taken nine years to build, was abandoned after fifteen years has never been resolved. Akbar's biographer merely says, disarmingly, that 'the pleasant palaces of that city did not engage his heart'. Lahore, where he moved, was better located for controlling the provinces of the northwest. There Akbar lived for twenty years, returning to Agra at the end of his reign.

Salim, named after Saint Salim Chishti, ascended the throne as Jahangir ('World Conqueror'). Contemporary paintings portray him standing delicately atop a globe, with a wistful King James I and the Turkish sultan looking up at him over the edge. Having inherited a stable and prosperous empire, Jahangir could devote his time to the things he loved best: paintings and gardens. Together with his accomplished and beautiful wife, Nur Jahan—the only Mughal queen to have taken a direct part in governance—he continued Akbar's tradition of patronising scholars and artists. At a time when Europe was embroiled in the Thirty Year's War, the court of 'the Great Mughal' had an almost fairy-tale effulgence to it.

Jahangir's son, Shah Jahan, had a penchant for white marble, and replaced much of what Akbar had built in Agra with buildings faced with marble; the shrine of Salim Chishti, likewise, was covered in a sheet of glowing white. The tragedy of his wife Mumtaz Mahal's untimely death was a terrible blow to the emperor. 'After this calamity, he refrained from the practice of listening to music, singing and wearing fine linen. From constant weeping he was forced to use spectacles.' His grief was sublimated by commissioning in her memory what became the most perfect example of Mughal architecture, not named after Mumtaz Mahal but known by its own name, the Taj Mahal (the 'Crown of Palaces').

Of Shah Jahan's two most likely successors, his sons Aurangzeb and Dara Shikoh, it was the former who out-trumped his brother and became effective ruler in his father's last years. Public sympathy has always been with the eldest Dara, a gentle scholar equally at home with Hindu scriptures and with Persian literature. By contrast, textbook writers have pilloried the somewhat austere Aurangzeb as a cruel bigot and speak of the 'decline of the Mughal Empire' after his death, almost as if it happened because of him. It is certainly true that the outpouring of creative activity in architecture patronised by the Mughals declined sharply in the 18th century, although painting and calligraphy continued to flourish. The interest in building moved off-centre, to the courts of Lucknow, Murshidabad, Hyderabad and Jaipur. The rulers of Bharatpur vandalised Agra to get dressed stone and carved sandstone to recycle for their own palace complex at Deeg. Luckily for Agra, it did not suffer invasion on the scale of the Persian ruler, Nadir Shah's attack on Delhi in 1739. In the later 18th century the Marathas, under their chief, Scindia, and his French military experts, controlled the city of Agra and its trade. In 1803, they were defeated by the British East India Company, who found Agra an excellent location from which to direct military expeditions into central India.

The Taj and the other great Mughal monuments of Agra have long been a focus for domestic tourists. Villagers from the extensive farmlands of Uttar Pradesh and the neighbouring states of Haryana and Rajasthan are occasionally seen arriving on flat-top trailers drawn by a well-used tractor or an overworked camel.

In the 19th century, Agra was a cosmopolitan city dominated by Muslim noblemen, Hindu bankers, French soldiers and British administrators. (Sherlock Holmes enthusiasts will be familiar with the 'Agra Treasures' in the *Sign of Four*). Agra, like most of the towns of the Doab, took part in the great Revolt of 1857. This meant that after 1858 the British army, both in the cantonment and in Agra Fort, was firmly in command of the city. It also meant that a railway line was built straight through the city, with a station each for the cantonment and the Fort. The unity of medieval Agra was broken and even the Jama Masjid was separated from the Fort by the railway line. But it was still regarded essentially as a Mughal town, as is evident from the building of St John's College, a brick-and-plaster imitation of Mughal architecture.

When he was governor-general, Lord William Bentinck was not above auctioning some of the marble from the Agra monuments, which gave rise to the story that he had planned to auction the entire Taj Mahal for its marble! It was left to a later viceroy, Curzon, at the end of the 19th century, to give these buildings the attention they

The Buland Darwaza, *built to celebrate Akbar's victory in Gujarat, leads the pilgrim from the village of Sikri to the great open courtyard of the mosque at Fatehpur Sikri. Salim Chishti's tomb is the focus of the pilgrim's attention.*

deserved. He catalogued his achievements with justifiable pride in his own initiative as well as in the work of the craftsmen:

> The Taj is no longer approached through dusty wastes and a squalid bazaar. A beautiful park takes their place...We have done the same with the succession of Mughal palaces in the Fort and the noble city of Akbar at Fatehpur Sikri...The skilled workmen of Agra have lent themselves to the enterprise with as much zeal and taste as their forerunners 300 years ago. Since I came to India we have spent upon repairs at Agra alone a sum of 40,000 pounds. Every rupee has been an offering of reverence to the past and a gift of recovered beauty to the future.

Little wonder, then, that the guides in Agra today answer most queries with the stock answer, 'It was done under Lord Curzon,' whether the question is about gilded ceiling ornamentation in Agra Fort or about the black buck gazing serenely in the gardens of Sikandra (Curzon, like some modern Noah, is supposed to have left a pair of deer and a pair of monkeys there).

In the great days of Agra, the Mughal presence ensured employment for innumerable masons, craftsmen, weavers, jewellers, soldiers and attendants. Today, too, people in the city follow these occupations. But the contemporary crowds in Fatehpur Sikri listen not to the cut and thrust of religious debate nor to the spirited recitation of poetry but to the drone of a guide who stands in echoing halls or on a dilapidated balcony, bravely seeking to convey what a Mughal city meant.

Today, the word 'Mughlai' brings to mind food, delicately flavoured chicken and biryani, just as the word 'Bourbon' denotes whisky. But there was a time when Agra and the Mughals conjured up a picture as vividly tinted as did the mention of Versailles and the Bourbons. The mystique of Mughal sovereignty was so strong that the East India Company, even when it ruled most of India, engraved the name of the Mughal emperor on their coins. The emperors had titles some inches in length, which for a time at least bore some approximation to reality. In the 16th and 17th centuries, the Mughals ruled over a vast territory. Administering and collecting land revenue from the *subas* (provinces) was a huge task. The cement of the empire was the loyalty of the feudatories and the imperial military power. Neither could be taken for granted: the emperors themselves travelled widely and frequently through their empire. It is said of the early Mongols that they even slept on horseback; the Indian Mughals were not very different—they were constantly on the move from one end of the empire to the other. It was in the intervals between these peregrinations that they built what is now known as Mughal Agra and Fatehpur. The description of their buildings as 'tents in stone' is apt; these citadels were the camps they pitched in some impulsive moment, camps liable to be just as impulsively broken.

The citadels, with their separate and airy buildings (Akbar is said to have built 500 palaces within Agra Fort, which were modified by his successors and, later, vandalised or destroyed by the Jats and the British) are a great contrast to the heavy edifices of European palaces, with their miles of echoing corridors. Given Agra's harsh climate, such buildings were ideal, equally amenable to letting in the sun as to keeping it at bay with barriers of damp and fragrant screens of *khas-khas* grass. Though the buildings were for the most part small and open, they were protected by formidably strong walls. Agra Fort's sandstone wall is 1.5 miles (2.5 kilometres) long, and in sections as high as 100 feet. Soldiers or cannon could not penetrate these unless aided by treachery. The cunningly angled gate and the barbican ensured that anyone entering the fort would be covered by the soldiers poised with their arrows behind the pencil-slits in the wall. Fatehpur, in the brief period that it was inhabited, was not stormed by any enemy forces; its very height would have been its defence, since in the unpolluted skies of those days it commanded a view of the surrounding countryside for miles around. It is a pity that the modern visitor does not always enter Fatehpur through the door leading to the Hall of Public Audience, or Agra Fort through the western (Delhi) gate. (The reason for the latter is that the army still occupies a large part of the Fort). The southern gate, in use today, is known as 'Amar Singh Gate', in memory of a Rajput prince who was killed here as he tried to escape after killing a nobleman at court. It is ironic that, although the emperors were carefully protected from attack, there was no way of defending them from those closest to them. One of the tragedies of the Mughals was that, except for Humayun and Akbar, the other princes showed anxiety and impatience to secure the throne. In the case of Aurangzeb, this went to the extent of confining his father in Agra Fort for eight years.

When staying at the capital, the emperor's movements were chiefly within the citadel—the city within the city. The emperor's highly disciplined daily schedule, imposed by the obligatory five daily prayers of the Islamic tradition, regulated the use of the buildings. His subjects had the satisfaction of seeing him briefly every morning, so that they could reassure themselves that he was alive and well. This was done by the emperor presenting himself at a *jharokha*, a small window, from where the crowds standing in the clearing beyond the Fort wall could see him. Shah Jahan, distressed that these people had to brave the sun and rain, ordered a 4-column pavilion to be set up in the meadow, to be covered with cloth. This no longer exists. If any subject wanted to address an appeal to his sovereign, it could be done during the sessions in the Hall of Public Audience (Diwan-i-Aam). When these sessions were in progress, drummers near or beyond the entrance announced the fact by a continuous tattoo. All officials and petitioners were screened and then allowed to pass within the citadel. In both Fatehpur and Agra Fort, the Diwan-i-Aam are large halls held up by numerous slender columns. Shielded by drapes and with carpets underfoot, animated with crowds controlled by the measured steps of court etiquette, these halls must have presented a scene of colour and sound difficult for the visitor to visualise today, standing in merely monochromatic spaces filled with echoing silence. It is equally difficult to imagine the open spaces beyond the halls—once ablaze with the colours of richly-ornamented elephants and gleaming horses, all lined up to show their paces.

The more secluded space of the Hall of Special Audience (Diwan-i-Khas) was where matters of policy were discussed by the sovereign, his ministers and senior officials. In Agra Fort, one must further use one's imagination to furnish the beautiful Diwan-i-Khas with candelabra, rugs and cushions, to refurbish the ornamentation on the walls, and to notice the tranquil backdrop of the river. In Fatehpur, the so-called Diwan-i-Khas seems an intriguingly unfunctional structure, although as a piece of craftsmanship it is a jewel. The curious central columns, linked in midair by narrow passages to the four walls, could not have been practical, since someone seated in the centre could not have communicated easily with the people sitting around him. Perhaps the building was meant for some specific kind of function, not for everyday use.

The routine of daily life was enacted both outdoors and indoors. It was easy to use exterior areas because the climate for much of the year was dry; the extremes of temperature and the searing winds could be controlled by appropriate architectural devices. Rooftops, balconies, and a wealth of gardens and pavilions, big and small, were available for formal and informal activities. An extra layer of space, refreshingly cool and dark in summer, was provided by the *tehkhana* (basement), a common

Although the materials used were very different, the floral motif was used extensively by the craftsmen working on Akbar's great city of Fatehpur Sikri and later at the Taj Mahal.

The Taj is first glimpsed through the arch of the great gateway to the south of the garden.

feature of homes in North India. Women had a clearly demarcated territory—the *zenana* was independent of the main palace complex and even had its own mosque. It has been surmised that the Jahangiri Mahal in Agra Fort was the *zenana*. Fatehpur is unique in having three palaces, said to have been for Akbar's three wives: one Hindu, one Christian and one Muslim.

The Mughals were not only 'World Conquerors' (Jahan-gir), 'Great Kings' (Akbar) and 'World Rulers' (Shah Jahan), they were also defenders of the Faith. The Agra Jama Masjid is, curiously, smaller in scale than the magnificent one at Delhi. Located across from the Fort, it was built by Jahanara, the daughter of Shah Jahan, in 1648, the year her father moved to the capital named after him at Delhi. The palace mosque, Moti Masjid ('Pearl Mosque') also has a namesake and a look-alike in Delhi's Red Fort. Akbar built a great mosque not at Agra but at Fatehpur, around the Chishti shrine. The mosque is not in use (unlike the Jama Masjid at Delhi), but the Chishti mausoleum commands the same devotion as do the older shrines at Ajmer and at Nizamuddin (in Delhi). Large numbers of devotees, Hindu and Muslim, offer prayers to the spirit of Salim Chishti with the same fervour as Akbar once did.

What makes the mosque at Fatehpur dramatically different from those at Delhi and Lahore is its entrance. We will never know whose was the amazing feat of imagination that created one of the most stunning views in the world—the Buland Darwaza ('Mighty Portal') atop a tall flight of steps that flows along the flank of the hill towards the great arch. It is a more dramatic and, considering the period in which it was built, an even greater engineering achievement than Paris's modern Arche de la Défense. It led into the mosque and the palace and out to the empire, for it symbolised the extension of empire by the conquest of Gujarat. Visual beauty, power, harmony, these are all there.

Akbar had his share of the restless curiosity of all of his family. In his case, it led him to listen to discourses on other religions than the one he was born into. The 16th century was a wonderful period when Hinduism and Islam found meeting ground in abundance, when Sufism shaded off into Bhakti cults, when Akbar's commander-in-chief was known by his title (Khan-Khanan) as well as by the name Rahim, which he used when writing poetry in Hindi. The Ibadat Khana, a building outside the Buland Darwaza that has not survived, was symbolically open to all points of the compass, and Akbar encouraged hours of debate between priests and theologians of all faiths—Hindu, Jesuit, Muslim and Jain. Always a daring man, he took matters further and propagated a new universalist doctrine (popularly called Din-e-Ilahi) with himself as the head of the new church:

> The mirrors of the inquirers of the age were polished. The whole of the night was kept alive by discussions which approved themselves to one and all. The degree of reason and the stage of vision were tested...and the lamp of perception brightened.

This new spirit did not last beyond Akbar but Fatehpur and its palaces embody its very essence.

Babur did not have only critical things to say about India. 'One good thing in Hindustan,' he wrote, 'is that it has unnumbered and endless workmen of every kind... 680 men worked daily on my building in Agra, and of Agra stone-cutters only; while 1,491 stonecutters worked daily on my buildings in Agra, Sikri, Biyana, Dholpur and Gwalior.' Babur and Humayun had laid out gardens and buildings on the left bank of the Yamuna. Akbarabad, around the Fort, was on the opposite bank. Akbar, a confident young ruler just out of his teens, engaged nearly 4,000 people to build his Fort. For an establishment that was most of the time peripatetic, the expenditure on enduring structures was of a staggeringly high order. Obviously the activity was deeply satisfying. In the inimitable words of Akbar's chronicler, the emperor 'gave expression to his heart and soul in the garment of water and clay', and 'in a short time there was a great city, and there were charming palaces. Benevolent institutions, such as schools and baths were also constructed and a large stone bazaar was built, and beautiful gardens were made in the vicinity...' Rajas and feudatories owing allegiance to the emperor bought or were granted land along the river. When Shah Jahan planned the mausoleum in his wife's memory, he bought a plot of land from the rajput, Raja Jai Singh I. He spent five million rupees on the Taj Mahal, for which task he assembled workmen from different parts of India, Iran and possibly Europe, who worked for 12 years.

The sterile simplification of Indian architecture into 'Islamic' or 'Hindu' categories ignores the richness and diversity that sparkles through Mughal architectural styles and decorative designs. Building traditions and idioms from Gujarat, Bengal, Rajasthan and Central India are all blended into a harmony that is ageless. What a lovely city Agra must have been with riverside gardens, terrace and canopies! Many of these survive only in place names, some in fragmented ruins. In 1861, when the Archaeological Survey began listing Agra's 'monuments', they found much of the ground 'strewed with fragments of glazed pottery—and old Delhi China'. A sad memory of past glory can be seen in the Chini-ka-Rauza, the tomb of a nobleman of Shah Jahan's court.

Today the palaces are bereft not only of their furnishings and illumination, but of the water that sustained life in this arid plain. Mughal buildings stayed close to the river, and always featured mechanisms for storing and distributing water. Babur is known to have commissioned a *baoli* (step well) in the local style. Fatehpur depended on a large reservoir, and one of the reasons suggested for Akbar's abandoning of it was the difficulty of getting water to the hill top. The gardens of Sikandra (where Akbar's mausoleum is located) and of the Taj Mahal, created in classical Persian style, remind us that the word 'paradise' is derived from *para daeza* (a walled garden). Channels of water around and inside buildings kept them cool in summer. To ensure that these green oases and these buildings were treated well, the rulers created endowments. For the Taj Mahal, Shah Jahan 'established an endowment consisting of the revenues of 30 hamlets yielding Rs1 lakh in revenue. Another Rs1 lakh was realised from the rent of bazaars and *serais*.'

In 1861, the Archaeological Survey was created by a contrite British government, uncomfortably aware that they had neglected and vandalised much of India's cultural heritage. Long before, the Mughals had shown how a conquering people can cull much that is practical and beautiful from the land they have acquired and from neighbouring cultures. Bishop Heber said of the Pathan kings that they 'built like giants and finished like jewellers'. Of the Mughals, we could say that they built their empire like giants and finished their buildings and gardens like jewellers.

Many of the floral patterns and designs used in the delicate inlay on the tomb and inside of the Taj are echoed on the decoration of the neigbouring buildings.

(following pages)
The earthy colours of the saris of visitors from western India contrasts with the white marble of the Taj. From its inception, the Taj complex was planned in a manner to make the movement of large numbers of visitors easy. The Mehman-Khana, *the* Karvan-Sarais *and the small township of Tajganj were intended to provide for the needs of visitors.*

(left) *The Taj buildings are situated at the end of a spacious* **chahar-bagh.** *The manicured lawns we see today are very different from the rich profusion of cypresses, fruit trees and fragrant flowers with which the Mughals loved to fill their gardens.*

(top) *Viewed from the east, with the River Yamuna flowing past, the scale and monumental greatness of the Taj Mahal becomes apparent.*

(bottom) *A late nineteenth century photograph of the Taj gateway.*

The Taj dominates the view from the
Mehman-Khana, *awesome in relation
to the people walking on its platform.
The great dome, luminous as a full
moon, plays 'hide-and-seek' behind
the trees and* (right) *at night glows
serenely while a Jaipur brass lamp
lights up the pietra dura in the arch
of the gateway.*

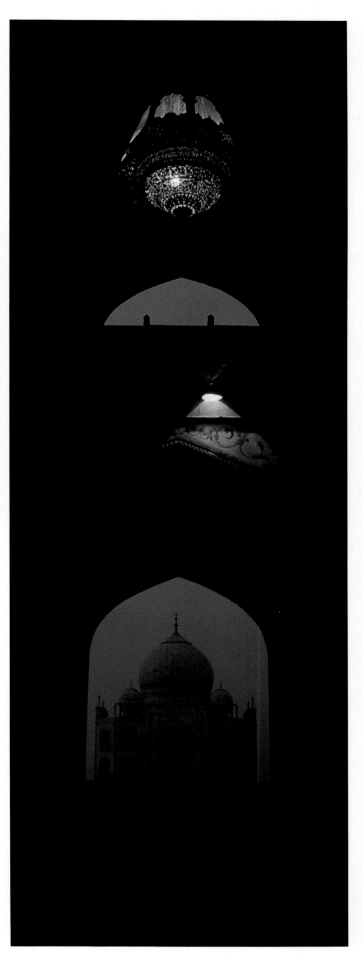

It took twenty-two years to build the Taj complex. The work was supervised by the experienced architects of Emperor Shah Jahan, Mir Abdul Karim and Makramat Khan who was also in charge of over-seeing the construction of the palace at Delhi. Some European art historians who could not bring themselves to accept that Asians could build so perfectly, convinced themselves that some European architect must have been the presiding genius. It is possible that the pietra dura work was co-ordinated by an Italian artist.

(bottom left) Two characteristic features of Shah Jahan's architecture-pinnacle terminating in a stylised bunch of flowers, popularly called a guldasta (bouquet), and perforated screens in marble, Shah Jahan's preferred stone.

The Mughal love of gardens found its way into their buildings. All the flowers they planted were immortalised in stone relief or inlay with a wonderful three dimensional quality.

(preceding pages)
The cenotaphs of Mumtaz Mahal and Shah Jahan are directly above their tombs. That of the Empress is in the centre. His tomb is bigger and more ornate, as is appropriate for an emperor. A screen encloses them with quiet dignity and the subdued filtered light invests the place with an appropriate solemnity.

The flowers in the hands of Shah Jahan and Mumtaz Mahal glow as brightly as the fresh flowers left by reverent visitors.

(following pages)
While the tombs of Emperor Shah Jahan and his queen are shielded many times, those of many others lie open to the skies, with only the feathery leaves of the keekar *trees to provide cover.*

More mosques were built by Shah Jahan than by any earlier Mughal ruler. The Jami Masjids of Delhi and Agra were built in his reign. The mosque to the left of the Taj Mahal is a smaller version of the Agra Jami Masjid, with three bays and the characteristic triple domes. Even here the flowers could not be kept from the external wall decoration, but the most distinctive feature of this, and the Mehman-Khana, is the restrained geometric designs using sandstone and marble, on the walls and in the dome's ceiling. The fine geometric pattens on the walkway around the base of the Taj echo the floral patterns used on the wall and dome decoration.

(following page)
The mirrored images of the Taj, in the slow waters of the Yamuna to the north and in the waterchannel to the south. are the most tranquil to be seen in Agra.

From afar one can be mesmerised by the complete sense of harmony that the Taj Mahal evokes. Having stood whilst the decades gradually pass, the monument is a testament to the evolution and power of the human imagination. With farmers tilling the nearby soil—as they have done for centuries—there is also a sense of humanity's ability to work in conjunction with nature. Though tourism is Agra's foremost industry, it is the land and agriculture that supports the majority of the population

(above) *As the morning sun lights up the sandstone of the Taj, the dhobis are busy washing clothes by endlessly beating them against slabs of sandstone, perhaps fragments of an earlier structure.*

The concern with the 'picturesque' led the British artists of the early nineteenth century to distort relative positions of buildings and to transfer the design of the ceiling of the Taj mosque on to the domes.

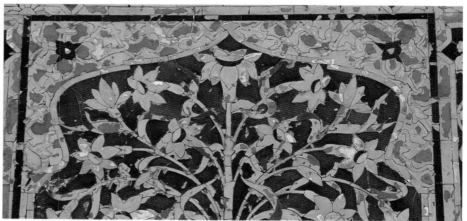

(preceding pages)
Babur, the founder of the Mughal dynasty in India, will be remembered for his gardens. His Aram Bagh set the pattern for other riverside gardens. This spacious walled garden is divided into quarters by raised walkaways. The pavilions overlooking the river have walls decorated with pictures of birds. To the right is an elaborate hammam (bathhouse) at basement level. Thus Babur compensated for two of the lacunae he noticed in India—the lack of gardens and public baths.

The Chini-ka-Rauza (mausoleum ornamented with glazed tiles) commemorates Shukrulla Shirazi, a minister of Shah Jahan. Glazed tiles had been used in earlier buildings to light up a dome or as bands along walls. But here it covered the whole structure extravagantly, a frozen garden interwoven with Quranic calligraphy. The interior was rich with painted stucco. Much of the enamel has been chipped off and the younger inhabitants of the neighbourhood have colonised it in the name of the "Dada Cricket Club".

Itimad-ud-Daulah was the title of a Persian minister of Emperor Jahangir, who was also the father of the Empress, Nur Jahan. She built this tomb for her father in 1628. Though much smaller in scale than the Taj Mahal, it anticipates and echoes its perfect balance and many of its features. Like the earlier mausoleum for Emperor Humayun at Delhi, it has a majestic gateway which veils the building.

(left) The theme of the marble tomb decoration is the flower, the symbol of hope and faith in the Garden of Paradise. One flower may be composed of dozens of delicately cut gemstones that trace the turns and twists of each graceful petal, the stamen and the leaves.

Set in a chahar-bagh, Itimad-ud-Daulah's mausoleum is a platform tomb with four corner minarets, like the Taj. The exquisite inlay work that covers all its walls was perfected here. All three mausolea are near the river Yamuna though only the Taj is reflected in its waters.

Akbar was just 14 when he began his rule, but by the age of 23 had launched himself into his first major architectural project.The year was 1565. The Akbarabad Fort was completed by 1569. Today, the pale pink sandstone still never fails to inspire awe.

(left) This 19th-century painting depicts the Red Fort on the banks of the Yamuna River. All the apartments overlooked the river and the rising sun. The emperors would travel to and from the capital, Delhi, by boat.

At the same time that the Taj Mahal was being built, Emperor Shah Jahan also added to and modified many of the buildings in the fort. In 1658, he was deposed by his youngest son, and it is said that he lived out his last seven broken years until his death (in 1666) under the care of his daughter. From the fort there is a compelling view of the Taj Mahal further down the Yamuna River. The Diwan-i-Khas was designed with cusped arches character-istic of Shah Jahan's beloved style.

The Fort's entrance is doubly fortified.
To Akbar's gateway, his great grandson
Aurangzeb added an outer wall a hundred
years later.

(opposite page)
The Shah Burj is an ornate marble tower
overlooking the Yamuna River. The protruding
platform afforded the gentle breezes floating
from the river the chance to sway and dance
through the marble screens.

54

(top) *Within the private area, the* Khas Mahal *of the Fort is a cluster of small airy buildings and the* Angoori Bagh *or Grape Garden. The Emperor's sleeping-pavilion,* Aram-gah, *is between two symmetrical buildings, the* Bangla *of Princess Jahanara and the* Bangla-i-Darshan. *The latter seen here, was used for the* jharokha-darshan, *when the emperor showed himself at the Palace window for the benefit of people gathered on the river bank below the fort walls.*

(bottom) *The Shah Burj, north of the Bangla-i-Darshan, similar to those in the forts of Delhi and Lahore, was where the Emperor could meet with officials in privacy.*

A carved marble pool and pietra dura pillar
in the Shah Burj unites it in style with the
Taj, which plays hide-and-seek behind the
columns.

(top) *The* Diwan-i-Khas, *Hall of Private Audience, links the public and private areas of the fort. The cusped arches repeat the design of the enormous* Diwan-i-Am, *Hall of Public Audience.*

(bottom) *A detail from the* Shish Mahal, *Palace of Mirrors.*

(top) *The* Bangla-i-Jahanara *derives its name
from the shape of the roof, which was
copied from the thatched roofs of Bengal
huts. Princess Jahanara, one of Shah Jahan's
daughters, attended to her father in the long
lonely years he spent in the Agra Fort as a
prisoner of his son Aurangzeb. The buildings of the Khas Mahal, with the dry basin
of the pool in front of the Angoori Bagh
echo the three buildings of the Taj complex.*

An old mausoleum has been 'recycled' as
a shrine to the monkey-god Hanuman.
The British cemetery also commemorated
the departed with marble cenotaphs.

(opposite page)
(top) *The rich offerings in a grocer's shop
in Tajganj.*

(bottom) *The tomb of Sarhindi Begum,
south-east of the Taj complex, is octagonal
in shape and is surrounded by a verandah
and encircled with slender pillars crowned
with* guldastas.

(following pages)
*A herd of blackbuck enlivens the spacious
gardens at Sikandra. Emperor Jahangir's
memorial to his father, Akbar, has a high
iwam decorated with coloured stone
skillfully set in a manner which makes
them look like tiles and flanked by domed
bays with painted plaster decoration.*

Sikandra is named after the Lodi ruler Sikander, but is on the architectral map because of the mausoleum built by the Emperor Jahangir for his father, Akbar. The tomb at Sikandra has many elements of significance: the extensive use of inlay work with marble and coloured stone to trace floral patterns as well as the more conventional geometric designs; its four minarets anticipate those of the Taj; the structure that stands in the middle of chahar-bagh is an unusual pyramid of sandstone pavilions surmounted by a marble storey.

The exterior and interior walls are covered with rich decorations like those on the borders of the miniature paintings Jahangir loved so well. The marble jalis on the top floor are each distinct in design, like the snowflakes of Kashmir, Jahangir's favourite part of India. The exquisitely carved marble tomb on the top storey is a 'false' one. Akbar's real tomb, in a solemn and simple setting, is on the ground floor.

Tinsel, pietra dura and marble have given employment to generations of craftsmen in Agra and Sikri. Age has not made any difference to the deftness of the hands carving yet another guldasta.

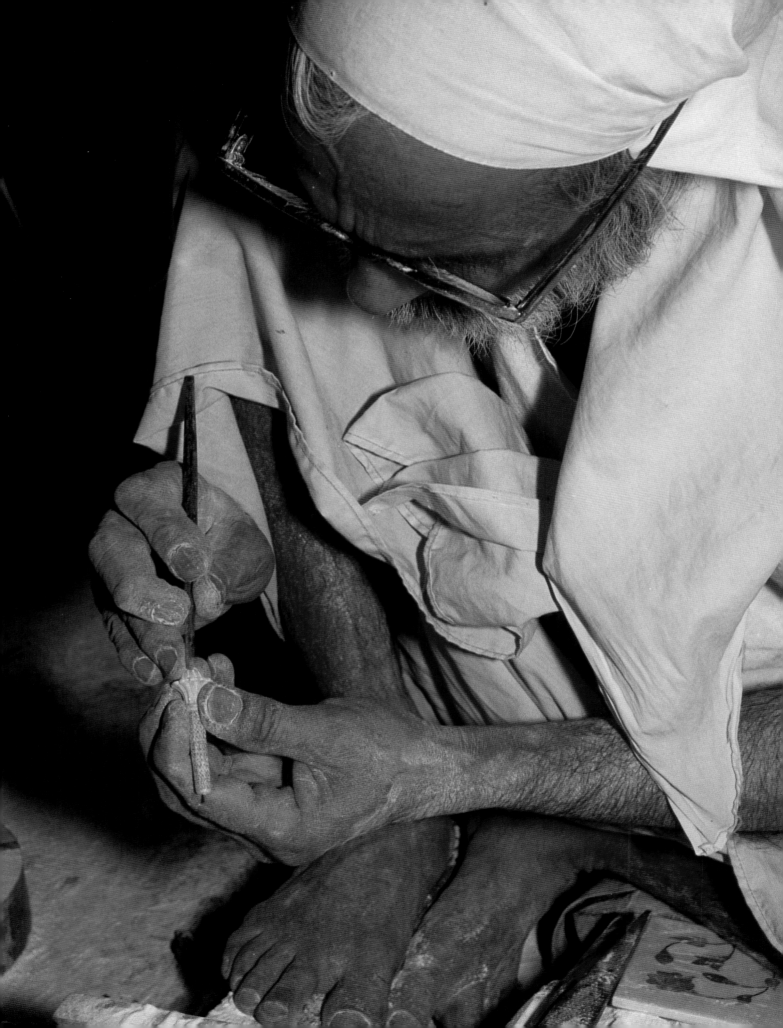

The bangles and necklace stall awaits
the visitors at the Buland Darwaza of
Fatehpur, while the vendor of spiced
snacks carries the ingredients of his
wares neatly packed onto one small tray.

(previous pages)
The Royal Apartments at Fatehpur Sikri,
a city of light and air, of palaces and
courtyards built by Akbar. The Mughal
architecture at Fatehpur Sikri necessi-
tated immaculate attention to details—
such as the glowing red texture of the
stone—designed to cultivate and
stimulate the senses.

Detail of sandstone and marble decoration.

(middle) *The village of Sikri seen through a broken arch of the old mint.*

(bottom)*"Urgent clothes can be laundered here". The clients are tourists now the Mughal courtiers have left!*

(above) *The verandah of the* Khwabgah, Chamber of Dreams, *looks out on the* Anup Talao, *a formal pool.*

Sandstone, the wonder stone, is plastic enough to be incised like clay, sharp enough to be cut into jalis and brackets and yet durable enough to last centuries. The central column of the Diwan-i-Khas *holds up a platform where the Emperor is said to have sat.*

In the spacious courtyard of Fatehpur's Jami Masjid stands the shrine of Saint Salim Chishti, whose blessings are said to have been instrumental in a son being born to Akbar. Fatehpur may have been deserted, but to this day scores of people visit the shrine to seek the blessings of the saint. From a height one can command a view of Fatehpur; the tank in front of the shrine. A little thread is interwoven with private prayers and tied to the jalis around the shrine.

Views of Jodhabai's palace.

Incense and flowers are sold near the Chishti shrine. The Panch Mahal, a five-storied pavilion, affords a series of terraces resting on columned halls, which was apparently used by the women of Akbar's court. Stone screens conceal those inside from public view.

An A-Z of Taj Mahal

A

Abdur Rahim Khan-khanan (1556-1627) was a commander in Emperor Akbar's army and subsequently prime minister to both Akbar and Jahangir. Gifted with a remarkable fluency in many languages, he translated Babur's *Memoirs* from Turki to Persian. He is best remembered and loved for the limpid verses he wrote in simple Hindi under his pen name 'Rahim'.

Abul Fazl (1551–1602) was a trusted adviser of Emperor Akbar. He was the author of the official history of Akbar's reign (*Akbarnama*) and a gazetteer (*Ain-e-Akbar*) and also, like so many in those spacious days, found time to write verse, under the pen name 'Allami'.

(The) **Archaeological Survey of India** was created in 1861 at a time when criticism was mounting against the wanton destruction by official agencies of many historic buildings in India. Sir Alexander Cunningham, the first director-general, and his successors, were men of great dedication, but what really made the survey effective as a guardian of India's architectural heritage was an Act promulgated by Lord Curzon in 1904.

Ashoka was ruler of Magadha (present-day Bihar) from 272 to 232 BC. His empire extended over much of India and Afghanistan. His edicts, inscribed on pillars and rocks, advocate dharma—Buddhist principles of religious tolerance, non-violence and social responsibility.

Aurangzeb (1618-1707) crowned himself emperor after defeating his older brother, Dara Shikoh, and imprisoning his father, Shah Jahan. He cultivated an image of austerity and dedication to his work. Unlike earlier Mughal rulers, he did not leave a legacy of art or architecture, but a digest of Islamic law.

B

Babur (1483–1530) was descended from two redoubtable warriors, Genghiz Khan and Timur. Court politics in the kingdom of Ferghana drove him to seek a new empire in Afghanistan and then northern India. His love of books and gardens was to be shared by his descendants.

Baoli This is a step well—a device for storing rain water in the dry regions of North and West India. Baolis are often many storeys deep, and schools or places of worship are usually built near them, making them a congenial place for congregation.

Bhakti is the concept of devotion or love in Hinduism, as distinct from ritualism. The attachment of a devotee to God is expressed through devotional songs in simple vernacular languages. The songs of the Bhakti saints (from the tenth to the 16th century) are still very popular. Surdas, Nanak and Kabir are among the best known saints.

Birbal was a close friend of Emperor Akbar, and was employed in various official departments. He was the only Hindu to accept Akbar's Din-e-Ilahi, and was known as a poet. There are many apocryphal stories portraying him as a man of ready wit and repartee.

C

Chahar-bagh is a feature of Islamic landscape gardening, where a square or rectangular area is divided in four by two axes forming a cross. The mausoleum of Humayun (in Delhi), of Akbar (in Sikandra) and of Jahangir (in Lahore) are set in the middle of such gardens. A variation can be seen in the Taj Mahal.

Chhajja is an Indian device of setting thin stone slabs in a building as overhanging eaves, to deflect rain or the glare of the sun.

Chhatri, a feature of much of the architecture of North India, is a small dome supported by slender columns, usually placed at the corner of a roof. It has a functional as well as decorative purpose, serving as a shaded place for sitting out.

Chishti is a Sufi order, with beliefs closely related to Hindu mysticism. It derives its name from the village in Afghanistan where one of its early leaders lived, and was introduced to India in the 13th century. Its saints include Nizamuddin Auliya (whose shrine is in Delhi) and Salim Sikri; their annual feast days are celebrated with great fervour by both Hindus and Muslims.

D

Dara Shikoh (1615–1659) was the eldest of the four sons of Emperor Shah Jahan, and his father's favourite. His religious eclecticism helped build many bridges of communication. The Persian translation of the Sanskrit *Upanishads*, which he commissioned, was later translated into Latin. His lack of military skill meant that he lost the battle of succession forced upon him by Aurangzeb.

Din-e-Ilahi (literally, 'the religion of God') was also known as Suleh-kul. Akbar urged his people to accept this monotheistic cult, which he devised to harmonise different religions—much as the Bhakti saints did. His followers had to be initiated by Akbar personally, but there were few takers and the cult did not survive him.

Doab (literally, 'two streams of water') refers to the area between two rivers, and is used to describe the Ganga–Yamuna plain.

H

Humayun (1508–1556) ruled the empire he inherited from Babur between 1531 and 1540, and again from 1555 to 1556. His throne was occupied for many years by the energetic Sher Shah Sur, an excellent administrator who is remembered for the highway from the Northwest Frontier to Bengal (the Grand Trunk Road). Humayun has been immortalised in the splendid mausoleum his widobuilt for him.

J

Jahanara (1614–80), the daughter of Emperor Shah Jahan and Mumtaz Mahal, was celebrated for her intelligence and her generosity. The *masjid* near Agra Fort is a tribute to her memory. She stayed with her father in his years of captivity in Agra Fort and spent her last years in Delhi. Her simple grave near the shrine of Nizamuddin Auliya is open to the sky, 'for such best becomes the sepulcher of one who has a humble mind'.

Jahangir (1569–1627), the son of Akbar and his Rajput queen, was named Salim after Sheikh Salim Chishti. A tolerant and humanitarian ruler, he patronised Persian and Urdu writers; painting reached a high point during his reign.

Jama Masjid is a large mosque intended to accommodate all the men in the local community for the most important religious service, held on Friday. One of the biggest in India is the one built by Shah Jahan in Delhi.

Jats is a community of agriculturists, including Hindus, Muslims and Sikhs, inhabiting the area from the Punjab to Central India. Characterised by a streak of egalitarianism, they own land not by individuals but by families. In the 18th century, a section of them took advantage of the weakening of Mughal power to establish a separatist state, with a fort at Bharatpur and a palace complex at Deeg. The latter was embellished with many things looted from Mughal palaces at Agra and Delhi.

Jaipur was built in 1728 by Raja Jai Singh II of Amber. Its regular layout was based on old Indian town-planning principles and its architecture combined Mughal and Rajput features. The rulers of Amber/Jaipur were on good terms with the British, since their ancestors had been with the Mughals. After independence, Jaipur became capital of the state of Rajasthan.

M

Mughal is a variation of 'Mongol' and is the name given to the dynasty of Babur, a Chagatai Turk, who was descended from the Mongols, Timur and Genghiz Khan.

Mumtaz Mahal (1592–1631) was the beautiful Iranian queen of Shah Jahan. A mother of 13 children, she died in childbirth.

N

Nadir Shah (1688–1747) was the Napoleon of Iran. Born the son of a shepherd, he rose to become a warrior and then, after deposing Tahmasp II, king of Iran. He invaded Delhi in 1739 and was acknowledged as overlord by the weak Mughal emperor. Indians remember him as the person who took away Shah Jahan's exquisite Peacock Throne. He died at the hands of a nephew who was ambitious to get the throne.

Nizamuddin Auliya (1236–1325) was one of the greatest Sufi saints of India. He refused to be involved in politics, and believed that helping the poor was more important than reciting prayers. His mausoleum is a place of pilgrimage for millions of Hindus and Muslims.

Nur Jahan (1577–1645) was the title of Mehrunnissa, the daughter of Itimad-ud-Daulah, a Persian nobleman. She was married to Sher Afghan and, later, to Emperor Jahangir. Accomplished and politically ambitious, she is remembered for the beautiful mausoleum she commissioned for her father, for the discovery of attar of roses and for the manner in which she dominated her easygoing husband.

P

Pietra dura is the elaborate inlay work of semi-precious stones used to cover a marble surface on all kinds of designs, geometric and floral. It was used in buildings in Rajasthan and was evolved to a new degree of perfection in the mausoleum of Itimad-ud-Daulah in Agra.

R

Rajput (literally, 'Sons of Kings') are clans that claim descent from the sun, the moon and fire. They are thought to have come to India from Central Asia in the early centuries AD. They were traditionally warriors and prized valour highly, ruling many city states in Western and Central India. In 1949, these joined together to form the state of Rajasthan.

(The) **Revolt of 1857** began in May that year, in Meerut, and was not completely crushed until 1859. Beginning as a mutiny by Indian soldiers against their British masters, it later drew in the civilian population of rural districts and some towns, including Delhi, Kanpur, Lucknow and Agra. The memory of it preyed on the minds of the British and created a divide between them and Indians; the latter mythologised the revolt as the 'First War for Indian Independence'.

S

Scindia is the name of one of the four families who were dominant in the confederacy in Maharashtra, which sought to establish an empire in the 18th century. The Scindia army was built up by a French general, de Boigne. In 1817, after the Marathas were defeated by the British, the Scindias were allowed to remain in their territory of Gwalior as dependent allies.

Serai is a building developed from the caravansarai of Central and West Asia—a shelter along highways or in towns for travellers and merchants. It usually consists of a large building with small rooms on all four sides of a spacious courtyard.

Shah Jahan (1592-1666) was the third son of Jahangir. During his reign, of which enduring monuments survive in Agra, Delhi and Lahore, the Mughals lost control of Afganistan but retained the Deccan. The *Shahjahan nama* of Inagat Khan gives a vivid description of the early years of his reign.

Sufism was a school of Muslim mysticism that developed over a wide area, from Egypt to India, between the ninth and 15th centuries. Its religious poetry emphasized a loving union between the devotee and God. In India the Chishti sect was the most popular, being characterized by elaborate ceremonies, music and philanthropy.

T

Tansen (d 1588) was a musician at the court of Akbar. Hindustani music was much appreciated and patronised by the Mughals. Even the austere Aurangzeb, who is supposed to have prohibited the use of music in public (giving orders to'bury it deep'), is said to have been a *veena*-player in his youth.

Timur (1336–1405) was born of a Turkish tribe in Samarkand, and was one of the great nomad conquerors. From 1381 to 1402, his armies cut great swathes through vast areas, from Moscow to Delhi. He died on an expedition to China. His dynasty, the Timurid, controlled central Asia and Iran until 1507. The Timurids were enthusiastic patrons of the arts, a tradition continued by Babur, who established a Timurid (Mughal) Dynasty in India.

Todar Mal (d 1589) hailed from the Punjab. He became Akbar's finance minister and worked out a land revenue system that endured a long time.

Chronology

1192	Il-bari Turks establish Sultanate of Delhi
1504	Babur occupies Kabul
1505	Sikander Lodi moves capital from Delhi to Agra
1510	Portuguese established in Goa
1526	Babur defeats Ibrahim Lodi at Panipat
1530	Death of Babur. Succession of Humayun
1540	Sher Shah Sur captures Delhi. Humayun in exile
1542	Birth of Akbar
1555	Humayun in Delhi
1556	Death of Humayun. Succession to Akbar
1565	The great empire of Vijaynagar in South India defeated by two neighbouring kingdoms
1565-70	Agra Fort built by Akbar
1569	Humayun's mausoleum at Delhi built
1571	Jama Masjid at Fatehpur built
1571-85	Palaces at Fatehpur completed
1596	Abul Fazl writes Akbar's biography
1600	East India Company granted charter by Queen Elizabeth 1
1605	Death of Akbar. Accession of Jahangir. Akbar's mausoleum at Sikandra
1615	Thomas Roe visits Agra
1622	Tomb of Itimad-ud-Daulah (Nur Jahan's father) built
1627	Accession of Shah Jahan
1631	Death of Mumtaz Mahal
1639	Work begins on new capital, Shahjahanabad, at Delhi
1643	Taj Mahal completed
1648	Shah Jahan moves to Delhi
1659	Accession of Aurangzeb
1666	Death of Shah Jahan
1707	Death of Aurangzeb
1757	British East India Company's victory over Nawab of Bengal at Plassey
1803	British conquest of Delhi and Agra
1857	The Great Revolt (the 'Mutiny')
1947	India gains independence

About the photographer:

Satish Sharma has been involved in some of India's most interesting and searching photographic assignments. For the last ten years he has undertaken a project photographing the street children and nomadic communities in and around India's cities. His coverage of the Ramlila celebrations at Ramnagar (near Banaras) was published in 1990.

About the author:

Dr Narayani Gupta is one of Delhi's leading historians. She currently teaches at the Jamia Millia Islamia University, New Delhi and the School of Habitat Studies, New Delhi. She has written numerous papers on Mughal history and the cities of Delhi and Agra. Her book "Delhi Between Two Empires" was published by Oxford University Press in 1982.